Grilling & Cookout Cookbook

An Easy Grilling Cookbook with Delicious Grilling Recipes and Side-Dishes

By
BookSumo Press
All rights reserved

Published by
http://www.booksumo.com

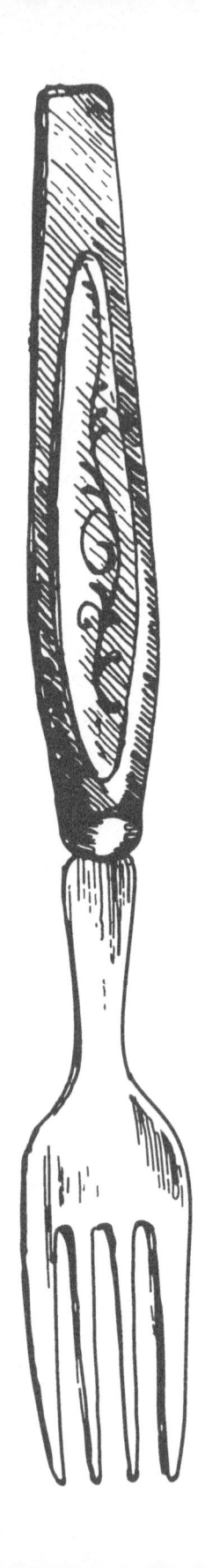

Table of Contents

Yummy Honey Chicken Kabobs 7

Grilled Salmon I 8

Apple and Shrimp Kabobs 9

Marinated Grilled Shrimp 10

Marinated Flank Steak 11

Grilled Bacon Jalapeno Wraps 12

Grilled Pizza Wraps 13

Spicy Shrimp 14

Shoyu Chicken 15

Grill Master Chicken Wings 16

Pretty Chicken 17

Grilled Mushroom Swiss Burgers 18

Grilled Spicy Lamb Burgers 19

Radishes On the Grill 20

Cabbage On the Grill 21

Asparagus On the Grill 22

Pineapple On the Grill 23

Beets On the Grill 24

Cauliflower On the Grill 25

Okra On the Grill 26

Avocados On the Grill 27

Bananas On the Grill 28

Peppers On the Grill 29

Tomatoes On the Grill 30

Asparagus On the Grill 31

Eggs On the Grill 32

Portobello Mushrooms On the Grill 33

Vegetables with Balsamic Vinegar 34

Potatoes On the Grill 35

A Salad of Asparagus 36

A Salad of Okra 37

Onions On the Grill 38

American Potato Salad 39

Egg Salad 40

Chicken Salad 41

Corn Salad 42

Maque Choux 43

Ensalada de Papas Colombiana 44

Tuna Salad 45

Macaroni Salad 46

Mesa Macaroni Salad 47

Kanas Style Fried Chicken Cutlets 48

Fried Chicken In A Japanese Style 49

Buttermilk Paprika Fried Chicken 50

6-Ingredient Fried Chicken 51

Chipotle Salsa 52

South Carolina Corn Cake 53

How to Make Tostadas 54

Aztec Corn Bread 55

Mayan Mashed Potatoes 56

Rocky Mount Rice 57

Charleston Chili 58

Brooklyn Style Hot Dogs 59

Mexican Multi Condiment Hot Dogs 60

BBQ Hot Dog 61

Mountain Time Hot Dogs 62

South Carolina Style Hot Dogs 64

Hot Dog Chili 101 65

Canadian Blueberry Pie 66

Southern American Pie 67

Old-Fashioned American Pecan Pie 68

Apple Pie 69

Southern Georgia Peach Pie 70

American Sweet Corn 71

Southern Corn Bread 72

Southern Corn Bread II 73

Caesar Parmesan Pasta Salad 74

Garden Party Pasta Salad 75

Fusilli and Mushrooms 76

Grilled Pasta Salad 77

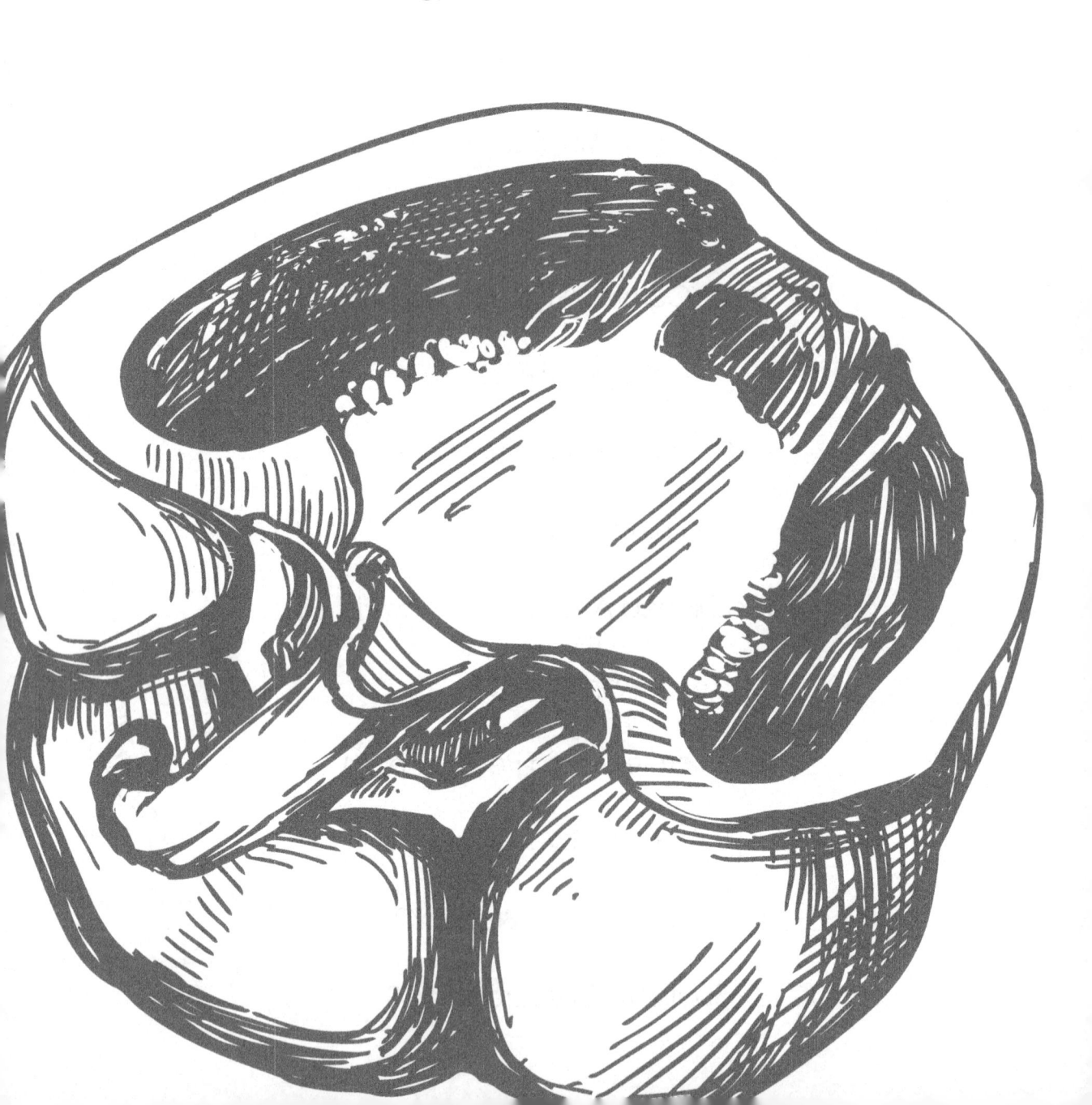

Yummy Honey Chicken Kabobs

Prep Time: 15 mins
Total Time: 2 hrs 30 mins

Servings per Recipe: 12
Calories	178 kcal
Carbohydrates	12.4 g
Cholesterol	45 mg
Fat	6.6 g
Protein	17.4 g
Sodium	442 mg

Ingredients

1/4 cup vegetable oil
1/3 cup honey
1/3 cup soy sauce
1/4 tsp ground black pepper
8 skinless, boneless chicken breast halves
- cut into 1 inch cubes
2 cloves garlic
5 small onions, cut into 2 inch pieces
2 red bell peppers, cut into 2 inch pieces
skewers

Directions

1. Combine oil, pepper, soy sauce and honey in a bowl, and add chicken, peppers, garlic and onions into it, reserve some of this mixture for future use.
2. Refrigerate everything for at least two hours.
3. You need to set grill at high heat and put oil over it.
4. Now remove every bit of marinade that you can from the chicken and put it on the skewers before grilling it for 15 minutes.
5. Serve.

GRILLED
Salmon I

Prep Time: 15 mins
Total Time: 2 hrs 31 mins

Servings per Recipe: 6
Calories	318 kcal
Carbohydrates	13.2 g
Cholesterol	56 mg
Fat	20.1 g
Protein	20.5 g
Sodium	1092 mg

Ingredients

1 1/2 pounds salmon fillets
lemon pepper to taste
garlic powder to taste
salt to taste
1/3 cup soy sauce
1/3 cup brown sugar
1/3 cup water
1/4 cup vegetable oil

Directions

1. At first you need to set grill at medium heat and put oil before continuing.
2. Put some salt, lemon pepper and garlic powder on salmon fillets.
3. Now combine soy sauce, vegetable oil, brown sugar and water in a bowl of your choice and put this in a sealable plastic bag along with the fish.
4. Refrigerate this for 2 hours at least.
5. Cook this on the preheated grill for about 8 minutes each side or until tender.

Apple and Shrimp Kabobs

 Prep Time: 20 mins
 Total Time: 1 hr

Servings per Recipe: 8
Calories   307 kcal
Carbohydrates   29.1 g
Cholesterol   213 mg
Fat   11.5 g
Protein   23.2 g
Sodium   247 mg

Ingredients

one tbsp chopped fresh basil
one tbsp strawberry jam
1/4 tsp crushed red pepper flakes
one clove garlic, minced
two tbsps balsamic vinegar
one tbsp lemon juice
two tsps white sugar

two Gala apples, cored and cut into eighths
16 jumbo shrimp, peeled and deveined

Directions

1. Mix honey, white sugar, basil, red pepper flakes, garlic, balsamic vinegar, strawberry jam, lemon juice and white sugar olive oil in a bowl very efficiently.
2. Now place apples and shrimp in a plastic bag and put the prepared marinade over both, and then seal the bag tightly.
3. Refrigerate for about 30 mins to get it settled.
4. You need to set grill at medium heat and put oil before continuing.
5. Thread shrimp and apples on soaked wooden skewers while discarding all the remaining marinade.
6. Grill the skewers for about 5 mins each side.
7. Serve

MARINATED
Grilled Shrimp

Prep Time: 15 mins
Total Time: 51 mins

Servings per Recipe: 5
Calories	273 kcal
Carbohydrates	2.8 g
Cholesterol	230 mg
Fat	14.7 g
Protein	31 g
Sodium	472 mg

Ingredients

3 cloves garlic, minced
1/3 cup olive oil
1/4 cup tomato sauce
2 tbsps balsamic vinegar
2 tbsps chopped fresh basil
1/2 tsp salt
1/4 tsp cayenne pepper
2 pounds fresh shrimp, peeled and deveined
skewers

Directions

1. At first you need to set grill at medium heat and put oil before continuing.
2. Combine garlic, balsamic, olive oil. Basil, cayenne pepper, tomato sauce and salt together in a bowl before adding shrimp into it and refrigerating it for at least 30 minutes.
3. Now thread this onto skewers very neatly, while discarding the marinade.
4. Cook this on the preheated grill for about 3 minutes each side or until tender.

Marinated Flank Steak

Prep Time: 10 mins
Total Time: 6 hrs 25 mins

Servings per Recipe: 8
Calories   275 kcal
Carbohydrates   3.4 g
Cholesterol   27 mg
Fat   22.5 g
Protein   14.8 g
Sodium   935 mg

Ingredients

1/2 cup vegetable oil
1/3 cup soy sauce
1/4 cup balsamic vinegar
2 tbsps fresh lemon juice
1 1/2 tbsps Worcestershire sauce
1 tbsp Dijon mustard
2 cloves garlic, minced
1/2 tsp ground black pepper
1 1/2 pounds flank steak

Directions

1. At first you need to set grill at high heat and put oil before continuing.
2. Combine oil, vinegar, lemon juice, soy sauce, Worcestershire sauce, mustard, garlic, and ground black pepper in a bowl before pouring it over the meat in a dish.
3. Coat it well and refrigerate for about 6 hours.
4. Cook this on the preheated grill for about 5 minutes each side or until tender.

GRILLED Bacon Jalapeno Wraps

Prep Time: 10 mins
Total Time: 20 mins

Servings per Recipe: 6
Calories   391 kcal
Carbohydrates   2.2 g
Cholesterol   79 mg
Fat   38.3 g
Protein   9.5 g
Sodium   577 mg

Ingredients

6 fresh jalapeno peppers, halved lengthwise and seeded
1 (8 ounce) package cream cheese
12 slices turkey bacon

Directions

1. At first you need to set grill at high heat and put oil before continuing.
2. Put some cream cheese to fill the space in jalapeno halves and wrap it around some bacon.
3. Use toothpick to hold it together.
4. Cook this on the preheated grill for about 3 minutes each side or until you find bacon crispy.

Grilled Pizza Wraps

Prep Time: 10 mins
Total Time: 30 mins

Servings per Recipe: 8
Calories 543 kcal
Carbohydrates 40.6 g
Cholesterol 69 mg
Fat 31.9 g
Protein 22.5 g
Sodium 1174 mg

Ingredients

4 oz sliced beef pepperoni
1/two cup pizza sauce
one (16 oz) package shredded Cheddar - Monterey Jack cheese blend

8 (10 inch) flour tortillas
two tbsps margarine, softened

Directions

1. At first you need to set grill at medium heat and put oil before continuing.
2. Spread some margarine over one side of a tortilla and with the margarine side down, place it over the grill.
3. Add one table spoon of pizza sauce, ½ cup shredded cheese and also some slices of pepperoni over this tortilla.
4. Fold it and cook it over grill until it turns golden on each side.
5. Serve.

SPICY
Shrimp

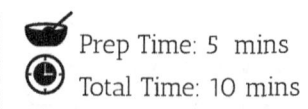

Prep Time: 5 mins
Total Time: 10 mins

Servings per Recipe: 4
Calories	101 kcal
Carbohydrates	2.6 g
Cholesterol	173 mg
Fat	1.1 g
Protein	18.8 g
Sodium	837 mg

Ingredients

one lb peeled and deveined shrimp
1/4 cup sriracha chili sauce
one tsp smoked paprika
1/2 tsp garlic powder
1/2 tsp onion powder

1/2 tsp chili powder
1/2 tsp ground cumin

Directions

1. At first you need to set grill at medium heat and put oil before continuing.
2. Mix shrimp with the mixture of paprika, onion powder, cumin, garlic power and chili sauce.
3. Put the shrimp on the preheated grill until you see that they are turning pink from the outside and the meat is no longer transparent which will take about 4-5 mins.

Shoyu Chicken

Prep Time: 30 mins
Total Time: 1 hr 30 mins

Servings per Recipe: 12
Calories	549 kcal
Carbohydrates	7 g
Cholesterol	67 mg
Fat	46.1 g
Protein	27.5 g
Sodium	1574 mg

Ingredients

- 1 cup soy sauce
- 1 cup brown sugar
- 1 cup water
- 4 cloves garlic, minced
- 1 onion, chopped
- 1 tbsp grated fresh ginger root
- 1 tbsp ground black pepper
- 1 tbsp dried oregano
- 1 tsp crushed red pepper flakes (optional)
- 1 tsp ground cayenne pepper (optional)
- 1 tsp ground paprika(optional)
- 5 pounds skinless chicken thighs

Directions

1. At first you need to set grill at high heat and put oil before continuing.
2. Combine soy sauce, water, garlic, onion, ginger, black pepper, brown sugar, oregano, red pepper flakes, ginger, cayenne pepper, and paprika in a bowl of your choice before putting chicken thighs into it.
3. Coat it well and refrigerate for at least one hour.
4. Cook these chicken thighs on the preheated grill for about 15 minutes each side or until tender.

GRILL MASTER
Chicken Wings

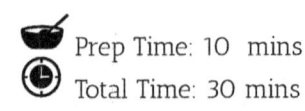

🥣 Prep Time: 10 mins
🕒 Total Time: 30 mins

Servings per Recipe: 6
Calories   181 kcal
Carbohydrates   2.3 g
Cholesterol   41 mg
Fat   14.6 g
Protein   10.1 g
Sodium   1154 mg

Ingredients

Wings:
1/2 cup soy sauce
1/2 cup Italian-style salad dressing
3 pounds chicken wings, cut apart at joints, wing tips discarded

Sauce:
1/4 cup butter
1 tsp soy sauce
1/4 cup hot pepper sauce to taste

Directions

1. At first you need to set grill at high heat and put oil before continuing.
2. Mix chicken wings, Italian dressing and soy sauce in sealable plastic bag and refrigerate for at least 4 hours.
3. Melt some butter and add soy sauce in a saucepan, and set it aside.
4. Cook these chicken wings on the preheated grill for about 25 minutes or until tender, while turning every now and then.
5. Pour butter sauce that you prepared over these wings.
6. Serve.

Pretty Chicken

Prep Time: 15 mins
Total Time: 4 hrs 30 mins

Servings per Recipe: 4
Calories	549 kcal
Carbohydrates	7 g
Cholesterol	67 mg
Fat	46.1 g
Protein	27.5 g
Sodium	1574 mg

Ingredients

- 2/3 cup olive oil
- 2/3 cup reduced-sodium soy sauce
- 1/4 cup lemon juice
- 2 tbsps liquid smoke flavoring
- 2 tbsps spicy brown mustard
- 2 tsps ground black pepper
- 2 tsps garlic powder
- 4 skinless, boneless chicken breast halves

Directions

1. At first you need to set grill at high heat and put oil before continuing.
2. Combine olive oil, lemon juice, liquid smoke, mustard, soy sauce, pepper, and garlic powder in a bowl before adding chicken.
3. Coat it well and refrigerate for at least four hour.
4. Cook this on the preheated grill for about 8 minutes each side or until tender.

GRILLED Mushroom Swiss Burgers

Prep Time: 15 mins
Total Time: 30 mins

Servings per Recipe: 6
Calories   520 kcal
Carbohydrates   25 g
Cholesterol   106 mg
Fat   32.4 g
Protein   30 g
Sodium   932 mg

Ingredients

1 1/2 pounds lean ground beef
1/2 tsp seasoned meat tenderizer
salt and pepper to taste
2 (4 ounce) cans sliced mushrooms, drained

2 tsps butter
2 tbsps soy sauce
4 slices Swiss cheese
6 hamburger buns

Directions

1. At first you need to set grill at high heat and put oil before continuing.
2. Take out the ground beef and divide it evenly among six patties before adding pepper, meat tenderizer and salt into it.
3. Cook mushrooms and soy sauce in hot butter until brown and set aside.
4. Cook patties on the preheated grill for about 8 minutes each side or until tender.
5. Now divide the mushrooms mixture evenly among all the burgers and also put one slice of Swiss cheese on top of these mushrooms.
6. Cover the grill for about 1 minute to melt the cheese before serving it in hamburger buns.

Grilled Spicy Lamb Burgers

Prep Time: 15 mins
Total Time: 25 mins

Servings per Recipe: 4
Calories	478 kcal
Carbohydrates	38 g
Cholesterol	101 mg
Fat	22.4 g
Protein	29.4 g
Sodium	1003 mg

Ingredients

- 1 pound ground lamb
- 2 tbsps chopped fresh mint leaves
- 2 tbsps chopped fresh cilantro
- 2 tbsps chopped fresh oregano
- 1 tbsp garlic, chopped
- 1 tsp apple cider
- 1 tsp white vinegar
- 1 tsp molasses
- 1 tsp ground cumin
- 1/4 tsp ground allspice
- 1/2 tsp red pepper flakes
- 1/2 tsp salt
- 1/2 tsp ground black pepper
- 4 pita bread rounds
- 4 ounces feta cheese, crumbled

Directions

1. At first you need to set grill at high heat and put oil before continuing.
2. Pour mixture of mint, cilantro, oregano, garlic, apple cider, vinegar, and molasses over lamb in a large sized bowl.
3. Now add cumin, red pepper flakes, allspice, salt, and black pepper into it before making four patties out of it.
4. Cook these chicken thighs on the preheated grill for about 8 minutes each side or until tender.
5. Serve burgers wrapped in pitas and feta cheese.

RADISHES
On the Grill

Prep Time: 15 mins
Total Time: 35 mins

Servings per Recipe: 6
Calories	51 kcal
Carbohydrates	3.6 g
Cholesterol	10 mg
Fat	3.9 g
Protein	0.7 g
Sodium	64 mg

Ingredients

20 oz radishes, sliced
two cloves garlic, minced
two tbsps butter, cut into small pieces
one cube ice
salt and pepper to taste

Directions

1. At first you need to set grill at high heat before continuing.
2. Now take out aluminum foil having a double layer and put radishes, ice cube, garlic and butter into it
3. Now add some salt and pepper according to your choice before sealing it tightly.
4. Place this foil and radishes on the preheated grill for about 20 mins to make radishes tender.

Cabbage On the Grill

Prep Time: 10 mins
Total Time: 45 mins

Servings per Recipe: 6
Calories   76 kcal
Carbohydrates   9.3 g
Cholesterol   11 mg
Fat   4.2 g
Protein   2.1 g
Sodium   115 mg

Ingredients

one head cabbage, cored
one tbsp butter
salt and ground black pepper to taste

one lb turkey bacon

Directions

1. At first you need to set grill at medium heat and put oil before continuing.
2. Cover cabbage with butter, pepper and salt.
3. Insert some bacon slices into the cabbage.
4. Place the remaining bacon slices over cabbage and wrap everything in aluminum foil
5. Grill the wrapped cabbage for 45-50 mins and cook the bacon on top of this cabbage.

ASPARAGUS
On the Grill

Prep Time: 15 mins
Total Time: 18 mins

Servings per Recipe: 4
Calories	53 kcal
Carbohydrates	4.4 g
Cholesterol	0 mg
Fat	3.5 g
Protein	2.5 g
Sodium	2 mg

Ingredients

one lb fresh asparagus spears, trimmed
one tbsp olive oil
salt and pepper to taste

Directions

1. At first you need to set grill at high heat before continuing.
2. Use some olive oil on the asparagus spears and also add some salt and pepper according to your taste
3. Now place asparagus over grill to make it tender for about 2-three mins.

Pineapple On the Grill

Prep Time: 5 mins
Total Time: 15 mins

Servings per Recipe: 12
Calories	46 kcal
Carbohydrates	5.3 g
Cholesterol	8 mg
Fat	2.9 g
Protein	0.2 g
Sodium	23 mg

Ingredients

one fresh pineapple - peeled, cored and cut into one inch rings
1/4 tsp honey
three tbsps melted butter
one dash hot pepper sauce
salt to taste

Directions

1. Take out the slices of pineapple and place them in plastic bag.
2. Now add some honey, salt, butter and hot pepper sauce over these slices.
3. Shake it well and marinate this for at least 30 mins.
4. You need to set grill at high heat before doing anything else
5. Grill these slices of pineapple for about 2-three mins each side.
6. Serve.

BEETS
On the Grill

Prep Time: 10 mins
Total Time: 45 mins

Servings per Recipe: 2
Calories   208 kcal
Carbohydrates   23.5 g
Cholesterol   31 mg
Fat   11.9 g
Protein   4.1 g
Sodium   467 mg

Ingredients

6 beets, scrubbed
two tbsps butter
salt and pepper to taste

Directions

1. At first you need to set grill at high heat before continuing.
2. Take an aluminum foil and brush one side of the foil with oil.
3. Now take out beets and some butter, and place it over the foil
4. Place foil and beets on the grill and cook it for about 30 mins to get it tender.
5. Let it cool down for 5 mins before serving

Cauliflower
On the Grill

Prep Time: 10 mins
Total Time: 35 mins

Servings per Recipe: 4	
Calories	81 kcal
Carbohydrates	11.5 g
Cholesterol	0 mg
Fat	3.6 g
Protein	2.9 g
Sodium	503 mg

Ingredients

- one head cauliflower, cut into thick slices
- one tbsp olive oil
- one tbsp brown sugar
- two tsps seasoned salt

Directions

1. At first you need to set grill at medium heat and put oil before continuing.
2. Put some seasoned salt, olive oil, brown sugar on both sides of cauliflower slices.
3. Put these on the preheated grill and cook it for about two mins each side before putting these slices into grill safe pan and cook for another 20 mins to get it tender.

OKRA
On the Grill

Prep Time: 5 mins
Total Time: 10 mins

Servings per Recipe: 4
Calories   156 kcal
Carbohydrates   11.4 g
Cholesterol   31 mg
Fat   12 g
Protein   3 g
Sodium   1501 mg

Ingredients

one lb fresh okra
1/4 cup melted butter
1/4 cup Cajun seasoning

Directions

1. At first you need to set grill at high heat before continuing.
2. Take out okra and put some butter and Cajun seasoning over it before grilling it for about two mins each side.
3. Serve.

Avocados On the Grill

Prep Time: 10 mins
Total Time: 15 mins

Servings per Recipe:	8
Calories	221 kcal
Carbohydrates	8.6 g
Cholesterol	0 mg
Fat	21.5 g
Protein	2 g
Sodium	8 mg

Ingredients

- 1/4 cup olive oil, or as needed
- one pinch ground chipotle pepper, or more to taste
- one pinch chili powder, or more to taste
- 4 avocados, halved and pitted

Directions

1. At first you need to set grill at medium heat and put oil before continuing.
2. Mix olive oil, chili powder and some chipotle pepper in a mixing bowl and put this mixture over the cut side of the avocado.
3. Grill these avocados for about 5 mins.

BANANAS
On the Grill

Prep Time: 5 mins
Total Time: 15 mins

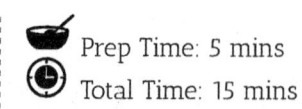

Servings per Recipe: 4
Calories	148 kcal
Carbohydrates	38.1 g
Cholesterol	0 mg
Fat	0.5 g
Protein	1.5 g
Sodium	3 mg

Ingredients

4 banana, peeled and halved lengthwise
one tbsp brown sugar
two tsps lemon juice
two tsps honey
splash of orange juice

Directions

1. Set your grill to high level of heat. Cover the grill with foil.
2. Cover your bananas with honey, orange, and brown sugar in a plastic bag for 10 mins.
3. Now place bananas on the grill while the fruit cooks add left over seasonings.
4. Grill for 5 mins.

Peppers On the Grill

Prep Time: 15 mins
Total Time: 15 mins

Servings per Recipe: 6
Calories	63 kcal
Carbohydrates	3.9 g
Cholesterol	12 mg
Fat	3.2 g
Protein	5.2 g
Sodium	308 mg

Ingredients

three green bell peppers, cut into large chunks
1/2 cup sliced jalapeno peppers
one pinch dried oregano
one cup shredded mozzarella cheese

Directions

1. At first you need to set grill at medium heat and put oil before continuing.
2. Take out the pepper pieces and place them over grill for about 3-5 mins with the inside facing in downward direction.
3. Now place some jalapeno slices in these peppers after turning over and also add some mozzarella cheese and oregano.
4. Grill pepper until the cheese melts and serve.

TOMATOES
On the Grill

Prep Time: 15 mins
Total Time: 25 mins

Servings per Recipe: 16
Calories 21 kcal
Carbohydrates 3 g
Cholesterol 0 mg
Fat 1 g
Protein 0.7 g
Sodium 149 mg

Ingredients

8 tomatoes, halved lengthwise
one tbsp olive oil
two cloves garlic, minced, or to taste
one tsp salt and ground black pepper to taste

Directions

1. At first you need to set grill at medium heat and put oil before continuing.
2. Put some olive oil, garlic, black pepper and salt over the cut side of the tomatoes.
3. Place these tomatoes over the preheated grill with the cut sides up for about 4 mins and then turn it over and grill for another three mins or until you see that the garlic is turning golden brown.

Asparagus On the Grill

Prep Time: 10 mins
Total Time: 18 mins

Servings per Recipe: 4
Calories   100 kcal
Carbohydrates   9.8 g
Cholesterol   0 mg
Fat   5.9 g
Protein   4.9 g
Sodium   230 mg

Ingredients

one tbsp toasted sesame oil
one tbsp soy sauce
three cloves garlic, minced
one tsp brown sugar

one 1/2 lbs fresh asparagus, trimmed
two tbsps toasted sesame seeds

Directions

1. At first you need to set grill at medium heat and put oil before continuing.
2. Mix asparagus with the mixture of soy sauce, brown sugar, garlic and sesame oil.
3. Now place this asparagus on grill and cook it for about 8 mins.
4. Garnish this with sesame seeds and serve.

EGGS
On the Grill

🥣 Prep Time: 2 mins
🕐 Total Time: 20 mins

Servings per Recipe: 6
Calories   143 kcal
Carbohydrates   0.8 g
Cholesterol   372 mg
Fat   9.9 g
Protein   12.6 g
Sodium   140 mg

Ingredients

12 eggs

Directions

1. At first you need to set grill at medium heat and put oil before continuing.
2. Coat each section of a muffin pan with some oil and add eggs evenly to each section.
3. Place the pan over grill for two mins or to your desired tenderness

Portobello Mushrooms On the Grill

 Prep Time: 15 mins
 Total Time: 25 mins

Servings per Recipe: 4
Calories	156 kcal
Carbohydrates	7.3 g
Cholesterol	0 mg
Fat	13.8 g
Protein	3.1 g
Sodium	589 mg

Ingredients

1/two cup finely chopped red bell pepper
one clove garlic, minced
1/4 cup olive oil
1/4 tsp onion powder
one tsp salt
1/two tsp ground black pepper
4 Portobello mushroom caps

Directions

1. At first you need to set grill at medium heat and put oil before continuing.
2. Take out a large mixing bowl and add red bell pepper, ground pepper, garlic, salt, oil and onion powder while mixing it thoroughly.
3. Spread mixture over the gill side of the mushroom caps.
4. Place these mushrooms over grill, place lid on grill and cook for about 20 mins.
5. Serve

VEGETABLES with Balsamic Vinegar

Prep Time: 15 mins
Total Time: 1 hr 10 mins

Servings per Recipe: 8
Calories   142 kcal
Carbohydrates   4.8 g
Cholesterol   0 mg
Fat   13.7 g
Protein   1.4 g
Sodium   380 mg

Ingredients

1/2 cup olive oil
two tbsps soy sauce
two tbsps balsamic vinegar
1/2 tsp salt
1/2 tsp ground black pepper

two eggplants, cut into 1/2-inch slices
three zucchinis, cut into 1/2-inch slices
two green bell peppers, cut into 1/2-inch slices

Directions

1. Mix together balsamic vinegar, pepper, soy sauce, salt and olive oil in a bowl and then put this mixture on eggplants, zucchinis and bell peppers before marinating it for about 45 mins.
2. At first you need to set grill at medium heat and put oil before continuing.
3. Remove vegetables from the marinade and put it on grill for about 15 mins while brushing these vegetables with the marinade.
4. Serve with the remaining marinade.

Potatoes On the Grill

Prep Time: 5 mins
Total Time: 27 mins

Servings per Recipe: 4
Calories   203 kcal
Carbohydrates   32.2 g
Cholesterol   0 mg
Fat   6.9 g
Protein   3.7 g
Sodium   108 mg

Ingredients

- two large russet potatoes, scrubbed
- two tbsps olive oil
- salt and ground black pepper to taste

Directions

1. Place potato in the microwave for about 5 mins on high heat and while turning it over halfway to get it cooked evenly
2. Slice the potato in two parts in length and cook for another two mins
3. You need to set grill at medium heat and put oil before continuing.
4. Put some olive oil, pepper and salt over the potatoes and cook it on the grill for about 20 mins while turning it when appropriate.

A SALAD
of Asparagus

Prep Time: 10 mins
Total Time: 14 mins

Servings per Recipe: 6
Calories	112 kcal
Carbohydrates	3.4 g
Cholesterol	2 mg
Fat	10.3 g
Protein	2.8 g
Sodium	57 mg

Ingredients

1/4 cup olive oil
1/8 cup lemon juice
12 fresh asparagus spears
6 cups fresh spinach leaves
1/8 cup grated Parmesan cheese
one tbsp seasoned slivered almonds

Directions

1. At first you need to set grill at low heat and put oil before continuing.
2. Coat asparagus with the mixture of lemon juice and olive oil.
3. Grill asparagus for about 5 mins, turning it often for even cooking and brushing it with the mixture previously prepared.
4. Now put it back into that mixture and add parmesan cheese, spinach and slivered almonds while cutting asparagus into small pieces.
5. Toss it well and serve.

A Salad of Okra

Prep Time: 10 mins
Total Time: 15 mins

Servings per Recipe: 2
Calories	50 kcal
Carbohydrates	11 g
Cholesterol	0 mg
Fat	0.2 g
Protein	2.9 g
Sodium	35 mg

Ingredients

1/4 cup white vinegar
one orange tomato, cubed
1/2 red onion, diced
16 pods fresh okra

salt to taste

Directions

1. At first you need to set grill at medium heat and put oil before continuing.
2. Prepare a mixture of vinegar, tomato, salt and onion in a bowl for later use.
3. Place okra on the preheated grill for about 5 mins and then toss it with the previously prepared mixture before serving.

ONIONS
On the Grill

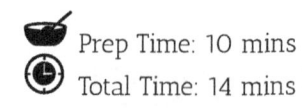

Prep Time: 10 mins
Total Time: 14 mins

Servings per Recipe: 8
Calories 136 kcal
Carbohydrates 7.6 g
Cholesterol 31 mg
Fat 11.7 g
Protein 1.3 g
Sodium 661 mg

Ingredients

4 large onions
1/2 cup butter

4 cubes chicken bouillon

Directions

1. At first you need to set grill at medium heat and put oil before continuing.
2. Peel the outer layer of the onion and make a hole on one side.
3. Fill this hole with bouillon cube and butter.
4. Now cover the onion in aluminum foil.
5. Now place these onions over grill for about one hour and then remove the top.
6. Slice them into small pieces and serve them with the juices from the foil.

American Potato Salad

Prep Time: 45 mins
Total Time: 1 hr

Servings per Recipe: 8
Calories	206 kcal
Fat	7.6 g
Carbohydrates	30.5g
Protein	5.5 g
Cholesterol	72 mg
Sodium	335 mg

Ingredients

- 5 potatoes
- 3 eggs
- 1 C. diced celery
- 1/2 C. diced onion
- 1/2 C. sweet pickle relish
- 1/4 tsp garlic salt
- 1/4 tsp celery salt
- 1 tbsp prepared mustard
- ground black pepper to taste
- 1/4 C. mayonnaise

Directions

1. Boil your potatoes in water and salt for 20 mins. Then remove the skins and chunk them.
2. Now get your eggs boiling in water.
3. Once the water is boiling, place a lid on the pot, and shut the heat.
4. Let the eggs sit for 15 mins. Then once they have cooled remove the shells, and dice them.
5. Get a bowl, combine: mayo, potatoes, pepper, eggs, mustard, celery, celery salt, onions, garlic, and relish.
6. Place a covering of plastic on the mix and put everything in the fridge until it is cold.
7. Enjoy.

EGG
Salad

Prep Time: 10 mins
Total Time: 35 mins

Servings per Recipe: 4
Calories   344 kcal
Fat   31.9 g
Carbohydrates   2.3g
Protein   < 13 g
Cholesterol   382 mg
Sodium   1351 mg

Ingredients

8 eggs
1/2 C. mayonnaise
1 tsp prepared yellow mustard
1/4 C. diced green onion

salt and pepper to taste
1/4 tsp paprika

Directions

1. Boil your eggs in water for 2 mins then place a lid on the pot and let the contents sit for 15 mins. Once the eggs have cooled remove their shells and dice them.
2. Now get a bowl, combine: green onions, eggs, mustard, and mayo.
3. Stir the mix until it is smooth then add in the paprika, pepper, and salt.
4. Stir the contents again then enjoy with toasted buns.

Chicken Salad

Prep Time: 15 mins
Total Time: 15 mins

Servings per Recipe: 12
Calories	315 kcal
Fat	23.1 g
Carbohydrates	15.2 g
Protein	13.9 g
Cholesterol	42 mg
Sodium	213 mg

Ingredients

- 4 C. cubed, cooked chicken meat
- 1 C. mayonnaise
- 1 tsp paprika
- 1 1/2 C. dried cranberries
- 1 C. diced celery
- 2 green onions, diced
- 1/2 C. minced green bell pepper
- 1 C. diced pecans
- 1 tsp seasoning salt
- ground black pepper to taste

Directions

1. Get a bowl, combine: seasoned salt, paprika, and mayo. Get this mix smooth then add in: the nuts, celery, onion, bell peppers, and cranberries.
2. Mix everything again then add the chicken and black pepper.
3. Place the contents in the fridge for 65 mins then serve.
4. Enjoy.

CORN
Salad

Prep Time: 15 mins
Total Time: 4 hrs 15 mins

Servings per Recipe: 8
Calories   201 kcal
Fat   13.3 g
Carbohydrates   18g
Protein   2.4 g
Cholesterol   5 mg
Sodium   340 mg

Ingredients

Dressing:
1/2 cup mayonnaise
3 small green onions, thinly sliced
2 tablespoons white vinegar
2 tablespoons minced pickled jalapeno peppers
2 tablespoons minced fresh parsley
1 tablespoon light olive oil
salt and ground black pepper to taste

Vegetables:
2 (11 ounce) cans shoepeg corn, rinsed and drained
1 cup halved grape tomatoes

Directions

1. Get a bowl, combine: olive oil, mayo, parsley, green onion, jalapeno, and vinegar. Work the mix completely then combine in some pepper and salt.
2. Now stir in your tomatoes and corn into the mayo mix. Place a covering of plastic on the bowl and put everything in the fridge for 4 hours.
3. Enjoy.

Maque Choux
(Native American Style Corn Salad)

Prep Time: 35 mins
Total Time: 1 hr 5 mins

Servings per Recipe: 6
Calories   211 kcal
Fat   11.1 g
Carbohydrates   22.8g
Protein   8.6 g
Cholesterol   14 mg
Sodium   371 mg

Ingredients

- 6 ears corn, husked and cleaned
- 2 tablespoons vegetable oil
- 1 large onion, thinly sliced
- 1 cup green bell pepper, chopped
- 1 large fresh tomato, chopped
- 1/4 cup milk
- salt to taste
- cayenne pepper
- 1/4 cup chopped green onions
- 8 strips crisply cooked turkey bacon, crumbled

Directions

1. Remove the kernels of corn from your ears into a bowl. Slice the ears again to get the milk into the same bowl.
2. Get your oil hot in a frying pan then combine in your green pepper, and onion. Stir fry the mix for 7 mins then combine in the milk, corn, and tomatoes. Stir everything then set the heat to low, and let the mix gently cook for 22 mins while stirring often. But do not let the mix get so hot that begin to boil.
3. Now add some cayenne and salt then set the heat lower and place a lid on the pan. Let everything cook for 7 more minx then add the bacon and green onions.
4. Enjoy.

ENSALADA de Papas Colombiana (10-Ingredient Potato Salad)

Prep Time: 20 mins
Total Time: 40 mins

Servings per Recipe: 8
Calories   124.1
Fat   2.0g
Cholesterol   0.0mg
Sodium   43.1mg
Carbohydrates   24.8g
Protein   3.1g

Ingredients

2 lb. red potatoes, cooked, peeled and cut into 1-inch cubes when cool
3 large carrots, peeled, cut into 1/2-inch pieces and steamed until crisp-tender, cooled
1/2 C. chopped red onion
1/4-1/2 C. chopped cilantro, depending on taste
3 large tomatoes, cut into 1-inch chunks

Salad Dressing
1/3 C. balsamic vinegar
1 tbsp oil
1 tsp seasoning salt (may add more to taste)
1 tsp sugar
1/4 tsp fresh ground black pepper

Directions

1. In a large bowl, mix together the potato cubes, carrot pieces, chopped onions and cilantro.
2. In a small bowl, add all the dressing ingredients and beat till well combined.
3. Place the dressing over the salad with the tomato chunks and gently, stir to combine.
4. Refrigerate to chill before serving.

Tuna Salad

Prep Time: 10 mins
Total Time: 10 mins

Servings per Recipe: 4
Calories	228 kcal
Fat	17.3 g
Carbohydrates	5.3g
Protein	13.4 g
Cholesterol	24 mg
Sodium	255 mg

Ingredients

- 1 (7 oz.) can white tuna, drained and flaked
- 6 tbsps mayonnaise or salad dressing
- 1 tbsp Parmesan cheese
- 3 tbsps sweet pickle relish
- 1/8 tsp dried minced onion flakes
- 1/4 tsp curry powder
- 1 tbsp dried parsley
- 1 tsp dried dill weed
- 1 pinch garlic powder

Directions

1. Get a bowl, combine: onion flakes, tuna, parmesan, and mayo.
2. Stir the contents until they are smooth then add the garlic powder, curry powder, dill, and parsley.
3. Stir the contents again to evenly distribute the spices.
4. Enjoy over toasted buns or crackers.

MACARONI
Salad

Prep Time: 20 mins
Total Time: 4 hrs 30 mins

Servings per Recipe: 10
Calories   390 kcal
Fat   18.7 g
Carbohydrates   49.3g
Protein   6.8 g
Cholesterol   8 mg
Sodium   529 mg

Ingredients

4 C. uncooked elbow macaroni
1 C. mayonnaise
1/4 C. distilled white vinegar
2/3 C. white sugar
2 1/2 tbsps prepared yellow mustard
1 1/2 tsps salt
1/2 tsp ground black pepper
1 large onion, diced
2 stalks celery, diced
1 green bell pepper, seeded and diced
1/4 C. grated carrot
2 tbsps diced pimento peppers

Directions

1. Boil your macaroni in water and salt for 9 mins then remove the liquids.
2. Get a bowl, combine: macaroni, onions, pimentos, celery, carrots, black pepper, mayo, salt, green peppers, vinegar, mustard, and sugar.
3. Place a covering of plastic around the bowl and put everything in the fridge for 5 hrs.
4. Enjoy.

Mesa Macaroni Salad

Prep Time: 10 mins
Total Time: 20 mins

Servings per Recipe: 4
Calories 534.8
Fat 24.8g
Cholesterol 15.2mg
Sodium 1501.3mg
Carbohydrates 72.7g
Protein 10.9g

Ingredients

- 2 C. small shell pasta
- 1 C. mayonnaise
- 2 C. chunky salsa
- 1 tbsp chopped fresh cilantro
- 6 green onions, chopped
- 1 C. cooked corn
- 1 C. sliced black olives
- 1 red pepper, chopped
- 1/2 tsp onion salt
- 1/4 tsp cayenne pepper

Directions

1. In a large pan of the lightly salted boiling water, prepare the pasta according to the package's directions.
2. Drain well.
3. In a large bowl add the remaining ingredients and mix till well combined.
4. Add the pasta and toss to coat.
5. Refrigerate to chill before serving.

KANAS STYLE
Fried Chicken Cutlets

Prep Time: 10 mins
Total Time: 1 hr 45 mins

Servings per Recipe: 10
Calories 481 kcal
Fat 21.5 g
Carbohydrates 49.4g
Protein 22.8 g
Cholesterol 65 mg
Sodium 6378 mg

Ingredients

3 C. cold water
1/4 C. kosher salt
1/4 C. honey
4 boneless skinless chicken breast halves
1/4 C. buttermilk
1 C. all-purpose flour
1 tsp black pepper
1/2 tsp garlic salt
1/2 tsp onion salt
cayenne pepper to taste
vegetable oil for frying

Directions

1. In a large bowl, add the water, honey and salt and mix till the honey is dissolved.
2. Add the chicken breast halves and coat with the honey mixture generously and place a heavy plate over the chicken to submerge it completely.
3. Cover and refrigerate everything to marinate for about 1 hour.
4. Remove the chicken breast halves from the marinade and pat it dry with a paper towel and transfer the meat to a bowl.
5. Add the buttermilk and keep it aside for about 15 minutes.
6. In a shallow dish, place the flour, onion salt, garlic salt, cayenne pepper, salt and black pepper.
7. Coat the chicken breast halves with the flour mixture evenly and arrange everything on a wire rack for about 15 minutes.
8. In a large skillet, heat the oil to 350 degrees F and fry the chicken breast halves for about 15-20 minutes.
9. Transfer the chicken onto paper towel lined plates to drain.

Fried Chicken
In A Japanese Style

🥣 Prep Time: 20 mins
🕐 Total Time: 1 hr 10 mins

Servings per Recipe: 8
Calories   256 kcal
Fat   16.7 g
Carbohydrates   4.8g
Protein   20.9 g
Cholesterol   98 mg
Sodium   327 mg

Ingredients

2 eggs, lightly beaten
1/2 tsp salt
1/2 tsp black pepper
1/2 tsp white sugar
1 tbsp minced garlic
1 tbsp grated fresh ginger root
1 tbsp sesame oil
1 tbsp soy sauce
1/8 tsp chicken bouillon granules

1 1/2 lb. skinless, boneless chicken breast halves - cut into 1 inch cubes
3 tbsp potato starch
1 tbsp rice flour
oil for frying

Directions

1. In a large bowl, add the eggs, gingerroot, garlic, soy sauce, sesame oil, bouillon granules, sugar, salt and black pepper and mix well.
2. Add the chicken cubes and coat them with the mixture generously and refrigerate, covered for about 30 minutes.
3. In a large skillet, heat the oil to 365 degrees F and fry the chicken cubes till golden brown.
4. Transfer the chicken onto paper towel lined plates to drain.

BUTTERMILK
Paprika Fried Chicken

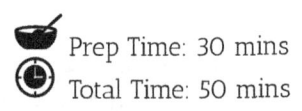

Prep Time: 30 mins
Total Time: 50 mins

Servings per Recipe: 8
Calories	489 kcal
Fat	21.8 g
Carbohydrates	29.5g
Protein	40.7 g
Cholesterol	116 mg
Sodium	140 mg

Ingredients

- 1 (4 lb.) chicken, cut into pieces
- 1 C. buttermilk
- 2 C. all-purpose flour for coating
- 1 tsp paprika
- salt and pepper to taste
- 2 quarts vegetable oil for frying

Directions

1. In a shallow dish, place the buttermilk.
2. In another shallow dish, place the flour, salt, black pepper and paprika.
3. Dip the chicken pieces in the buttermilk completely and coat them in the flour mixture.
4. Arrange the chicken pieces on a baking dish and cover with wax paper and keep aside till flour becomes pasty.
5. In a large cast iron skillet, heat the vegetable oil and fry the chicken pieces till browned.
6. Reduce the heat and cook, covered for about 30 minutes.
7. Uncover and increase the heat and cook till crispy.
8. Transfer the chicken pieces onto paper towel lined plates to drain.

6-Ingredient Fried Chicken

🥣 Prep Time: 15 mins
🕐 Total Time: 35 mins

Servings per Recipe: 6
Calories   491 kcal
Fat   32 g
Carbohydrates   16.1g
Protein   32.8 g
Cholesterol   97 mg
Sodium   94 mg

Ingredients

1 (3 lb.) whole chicken, cut into pieces
1 C. all-purpose flour
salt to taste
ground black pepper to taste
1 tsp paprika
1 quart vegetable oil for frying

Directions

1. In a shallow dish, place the flour.
2. Sprinkle the chicken pieces with salt, paprika and black pepper and roll them in the flour evenly.
3. In a large skillet, heat the oil to 365 degrees F.
4. Add the chicken pieces and cook, covered for about 15-20 minutes, flipping once half way.
5. Transfer the chicken pieces onto paper towel lined plates to drain.

CHIPOTLE
Salsa

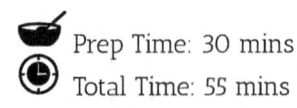

🥣 Prep Time: 30 mins
🕐 Total Time: 55 mins

Servings per Recipe: 6
Calories   198 kcal
Fat   14.8 g
Carbohydrates   17g
Protein   3.3 g
Cholesterol   0 mg
Sodium   82 mg

Ingredients

2 ears corn on the cob, husks and silk removed
2 tomatoes, chopped
2 avocados - peeled, pitted, and diced
1/2 bunch cilantro, stems cut off and leaves chopped

1 white onion, chopped
3 tablespoons chopped garlic
2 tablespoons olive oil
2 tablespoons balsamic vinegar
kosher salt to taste

Directions

1. Get an outdoor grill hot and coat the grate with oil.
2. Place your corn on the grate once the grill is hot and cook the corn for 4 mins each side. Turn the ears constantly to avoid any burning. After you have completely grilled the corn slice off the kernel into a bowl. Let the kernel sit until they have lost their heat.
3. Once the corn has cooled off combine in the: red vinegar, tomatoes, olive oil, avocados, garlic, white onion, and cilantro. Toss everything then combine in the kosher salt and toss everything again.
4. Enjoy.

South Carolina Corn Cake

Prep Time: 15 mins
Total Time: 1 hr 15 mins

Servings per Recipe: 6
Calories   273 kcal
Fat   18.1 g
Carbohydrates   27.9 g
Protein   2.6 g
Cholesterol   47 mg
Sodium   257 mg

Ingredients

1/2 cup butter, softened
1/3 cup masa harina
1/4 cup water
1 1/2 cups frozen whole-kernel corn, thawed
1/4 cup cornmeal
1/3 cup white sugar

2 tablespoons heavy whipping cream
1/4 teaspoon salt
1/2 teaspoon baking powder

Directions

1. Set your oven to 350 degrees before doing anything else.
2. Get a bowl, and whisk your butter in it until the butter is soft and creamy. Combine in the water, and corn flour, and continue to whisk everything.
3. Add your corn to a blender and pulse the corn until it is chopped evenly and chunky. Then combine it with the butter mix.
4. Get a 2nd bowl, combine: baking powder, cornmeal, salt, sugar, and cream. Combine this with your processed corn and stir then enter everything into an 8 x 8 dish.
5. Place a covering of foil on the dish and put the smaller dish into a casserole dish. Fill about 75% of the casserole dish with some water and cook everything in the oven for 1 hr.
6. Enjoy.

HOW TO MAKE
Tostadas

🥣 Prep Time: 20 mins
🕐 Total Time: 20 mins

Servings per Recipe: 8
Calories   252 kcal
Fat   11.3 g
Carbohydrates   27g
Protein   12.1 g
Cholesterol   34 mg
Sodium   945 mg

Ingredients

8 (6 inch) Old El Paso(R) Flour Tortillas for Soft Tacos & Fajitas
1 (11 ounce) can Green Giant(R) Steam Crisp(R) Mexicorn(R) whole kernel corn with red and green peppers, drained
1 1/2 cups shredded cooked chicken
1 (16 ounce) jar Old El Paso(R) Salsa (any variety)
1/2 cup sour cream
1 tablespoon milk, or as needed
2 1/2 cups shredded lettuce
1 cup shredded Cheddar or Monterey Jack cheese
1/4 cup sliced green onions

Directions

1. Set your oven to 375 degrees before doing anything else.
2. Lay your tortillas in a casserole dish and cook them in the oven for 11 mins.
3. At the same time add your salsa, chicken, and corn to pot and let it cook for 4 mins with a high level of heat while stirring.
4. Get a bowl, combine: milk and sour cream.
5. Once your tortillas are done baking cover them with the chicken mix and some lettuce then cheese. Top everything with the milk mix then green onions.
6. Enjoy.

Aztec Corn Bread

🥣 Prep Time: 30 mins
🕐 Total Time: 55 mins

Servings per Recipe: 9
Calories	220 kcal
Fat	8.8 g
Carbohydrates	29.3g
Protein	6 g
Cholesterol	61 mg
Sodium	422 mg

Ingredients

- 4 slices turkey bacon
- 5 tablespoons maple syrup, divided, plus additional for serving (optional)
- 1 cup yellow cornmeal
- 3/4 cup all-purpose flour
- 2 1/2 teaspoons baking powder
- 1/2 teaspoon salt
- 1 cup milk
- 2 eggs
- 1/4 cup butter, melted
- Reynolds(R) Bakeware Bacon Pan
- Reynolds(R) Bakeware Pan

Directions

1. Set your oven to 400 degrees before doing anything else.
2. Place your pieces of bacon into a baking dish and cook them in the oven for 10 mins. Add in 1 tbsp of maple syrup over the bacon evenly then let the pieces cook for 3 more mins. Once the pieces have cooled off chopped them.
3. Get a bowl, combine: salt, cornmeal, baking powder, and flour.
4. Get a 2nd bowl, combine butter, the rest of the maple syrup (4 tbsps), eggs, and milk. Whisk this mix together completely then combine both bowls evenly.
5. Stir in the bacon then combine everything.
6. Pour the entire mix into a casserole dish and cook everything for 22 mins.
7. Top the corn bread with some more honey if you like.
8. Enjoy.

MAYAN
Mashed Potatoes

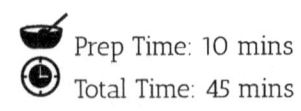

Prep Time: 10 mins
Total Time: 45 mins

Servings per Recipe: 5
Calories   439 kcal
Fat   30.8 g
Carbohydrates   39.2g
Protein   6.2 g
Cholesterol   81 mg
Sodium   595 mg

Ingredients

1 1/2 pounds new potatoes, scrubbed and quartered
1/4 teaspoon salt
1/2 cup butter, softened
1/2 cup heavy cream
salt and pepper to taste
1 tablespoon olive oil
1 1/2 cups whole kernel corn
1 (10 ounce) package fresh spinach, stems removed
1 1/2 teaspoons minced garlic

Directions

1. Get your potatoes boiling in water then add in 1/4 tsp of salt.
2. Let the potatoes boil for 17 mins then remove all the liquid and mash the potatoes with a masher then mash in the heavy cream and butter then add in the pepper and salt.
3. Get your olive oil hot in frying pan then begin to stir fry your corn in the oil for 4 mins then combine in the garlic and spinach and let everything cook for 60 secs then.
4. Combine this mix with the mashed potatoes.
5. Enjoy.

Rocky Mount Rice

Prep Time: 15 mins
Total Time: 1 hr 20 mins

Servings per Recipe: 8
Calories   331 kcal
Fat   10.1 g
Carbohydrates   51.9g
Protein   8.1 g
Cholesterol   14 mg
Sodium   1388 mg

Ingredients

- 2 C. uncooked long-grain white rice
- 6 C. boiling water
- 1 tbsp salt
- 6 slices turkey bacon
- 2 onions, chopped
- 1 (8 oz.) can tomato sauce
- 1 (6 oz.) can tomato paste
- 1 tbsp white sugar
- 2 tsp Worcestershire sauce
- 1 dash hot pepper sauce

Directions

1. Set your oven to 325 degrees F before doing anything else and grease a 2-quart baking dish.
2. In a pan, add the rice, water and salt and bring to a boil.
3. Reduce the heat to medium-low and simmer, covered for about 20-25 minutes.
4. Meanwhile, heat a large skillet on medium-high heat and cook the bacon for about 10 minutes, turning occasionally.
5. Transfer the bacon onto a paper towel lined plate to drain and then crumble it.
6. Drain the grease, reserving about 1 tbsp in the skillet and reduce the heat to medium.
7. In the same skillet, cook the onions for about 5-8 minutes.
8. Stir in the crumbled bacon, tomato sauce, tomato paste, sugar, Worcestershire sauce and hot sauce and bring to a gentle boil.
9. Reduce the heat and simmer for about 10 minutes.
10. Place the cooked rice and bacon mixture into the prepared baking dish and stir to combine.
11. Cover the dish and cook in the oven for about 45 minutes.

CHARLESTON
Chili

Prep Time: 15 mins
Total Time: 3 hrs 45 mins

Servings per Recipe: 12
Calories	389 kcal
Fat	18.1 g
Carbohydrates	34g
Protein	25.7 g
Cholesterol	57 mg
Sodium	1001 mg

Ingredients

- 2 1/2 lb. ground beef
- 3 tbsp olive oil
- 3 stalks celery, diced
- 2 large onions, diced
- 2 cloves garlic, minced
- 1 (29 oz.) can tomato sauce
- 1 (28 oz.) can crushed tomatoes
- 1 (6 oz.) can mushrooms, drained
- 1 1/2 C. beef broth
- 2 (16 oz.) cans chili beans, drained
- 1 (15 oz.) can kidney beans, drained
- 1 tbsp ground cumin
- 1/4 C. chili powder
- 2 tsp ground coriander
- 2 tsp cayenne pepper
- 1 dash Worcestershire sauce

Directions

1. Heat a large skillet on medium heat and cook the beef till browned completely.
2. Drain the excess grease from the skillet.
3. In a large pan, heat the oil on medium heat and sauté the celery, onions and garlic till the onion becomes translucent.
4. Stir in the coked beef and remaining ingredients and bring to a gentle simmer.
5. Reduce the heat to low and simmer for about 3 hours.

Brooklyn Style Hot Dogs

Prep Time: 5 mins
Total Time: 15 mins

Servings per Recipe: 8
Calories 276.9
Fat 15.3g
Cholesterol 23.8mg
Sodium 1071.3mg
Carbohydrates 24.6g
Protein 9.5g

Ingredients

2 dill pickles, chopped
1 (4 oz.) cans diced green chilies
2 tbsp onions, chopped
2 tbsp yellow mustard

8 kosher hot dogs, your favorite brand
8 hot dog buns

Directions

1. Set your grill and lightly, grease the grill grate.
2. In a bowl, mix together the pickles, chilies, onion and mustard.
3. Cook the hot dogs on the grill till desired doneness.
4. Arrange the hot dogs over the bun and top with the pickle mixture.

MEXICAN
Multi Condiment Hot Dogs

Prep Time: 15 mins
Total Time: 23 mins

Servings per Recipe: 1
Calories   320.3
Fat   18.8g
Cholesterol   29.2mg
Sodium   788.7mg
Carbohydrates 26.5g
Protein   10.6g

Ingredients

4 kosher hot dogs
4 hot dog buns, Hamburger
4 slices turkey bacon
1 large tomatoes, chopped
1 small onion, chopped
1 jalapeno, seeded and diced (optional)
1 tbsp cilantro, chopped
OPTIONAL CONDIMENTS
ketchup (optional)

mustard (optional)
mayonnaise (optional)
relish (optional)
cheese sauce (optional)
lettuce, shredded (optional)

Directions

1. Set your grill for medium-high heat and lightly, grease the grill grate.
2. In a bowl, mix together the chopped tomato, onion, cilantro and jalapeño and keep aside.
3. With the bacon, wrap the hot dogs and then secure with a tooth pick.
4. Warm the hot dog buns and wrap in a foil.
5. Cook the hot dogs onto grill till desired crispness, flipping occasionally.
6. Serve on buns with your desired toppings.

BBQ Hot Dog

Prep Time: 10 mins
Total Time: 17 mins

Servings per Recipe: 2
Calories   748.1
Fat   47.0g
Cholesterol   88.2mg
Sodium   1750.5mg
Carbohydrates   52.1g
Protein   28.0g

Ingredients

4 kosher hot dogs
4 hot dog buns
4 -6 slices turkey bacon, fried and crumbled
1/2 C. Walla Walla onion, chopped
1/2 C. sharp cheddar cheese, shredded
1/2 C. tomatoes, diced
barbecue sauce
1 jalapeno pepper, seeded and diced (optional)

Directions

1. Cook the hot dogs on grill till desired doneness.
2. Toast the buns and top with the sauce, followed by the dog, cheese, bacon, onions and tomatoes.
3. Serve immediately.

MOUNTAIN TIME
Hot Dogs

Prep Time: 10 mins
Total Time: 20 mins

Servings per Recipe: 4
Calories 330.1
Fat 20.0g
Cholesterol 33.0mg
Sodium 1070.4mg
Carbohydrates 25.5g
Protein 11.4g

Ingredients

1 tsp ketchup
1 tsp Dijon mustard
4 large kosher hot dogs
1/2 oz. cheddar cheese, cut into long sticks
2 tbsp chopped onions
1 C. refrigerated sauerkraut, squeeze to drain, roughly chopped
4 slices turkey bacon

vegetable oil
4 long hot dog buns

Directions

1. Set your grill for direct medium heat and lightly, grease the grill grate.
2. In a bowl, mix together the ketchup and mustard.
3. In another bowl, mix together the sauerkraut and chopped onion.
4. Split open the hot dogs, down the center, lengthwise, forming a deep pocket in each, but not cutting all the way through.
5. Coat the inside of each hot dog with the mustard ketchup mixture.
6. Arrange a cheese strip deep within each hot dog pocket and top with the sauerkraut and onions.
7. Encapsulate the cheese with the sauerkraut mixture at the ends as well, so that no cheese is exposed.
8. Wrap each stuffed hot dog with a bacon strip and secure with the toothpicks at each end.
9. Place the stuffed hot dogs on the grill, stuffing side down.
10. Cook the hot dogs, stuffing side down on the grill for about 2 minutes per side.
11. Flip the hot dogs a quarter turn and cook on grill for a couple of minutes, covering the grill in between and flipping.

12. During the last minute of cooking, open up the hot dog buns and place them open-side down on the grill till toasted lightly.
13. Transfer the hot dogs and buns onto a plate.
14. Remove the toothpicks from the hot dogs and arrange on the buns and serve.

SOUTH CAROLINA
Style Hot Dogs

Prep Time: 20 mins
Total Time: 4 hrs 20 mins

Servings per Recipe: 8
Calories   289.3
Fat   15.2g
Cholesterol   23.8mg
Sodium   806.0mg
Carbohydrates   27.5g
Protein   9.9g

Ingredients

8 all kosher hot dogs
8 hot dog buns, steamed
3 C. shredded green cabbage
1 small carrot, grated
1/4 C. red onion, diced
1/4 C. sun-dried tomato, julienne cut
1 C. mayonnaise (light is fine)

1/4 C. balsamic vinegar, plus
1 tbsp balsamic vinegar
2 tbsp tomato ketchup
salt and pepper

Directions

1. For the dressing, in a small bowl mix together the mayonnaise and balsamic vinegar.
2. In a large bowl, mix together the cabbage, carrot, red onion and sun dried tomatoes.
3. Add enough of the dressing and mix till the cabbage mixture moistens.
4. Add the ketchup and mix well.
5. Stir in the salt and pepper and refrigerate for about 4-5 hours.
6. Boil the hot dogs in boiling water and then drain.
7. Arrange 1 hot dog in steamed bun and top with the generous amounts of slaw.

Hot Dog Chili 101

Prep Time: 10 mins
Total Time: 40 mins

Servings per Recipe: 6
Calories   410.9
Fat   11.8g
Cholesterol   73.7mg
Sodium   921.0mg
Carbohydrates   52.4g
Protein   25.5g

Ingredients

- 1 large onion, chopped
- 1 1/2 lbs lean ground beef
- 1 (32 oz.) cans tomato puree
- 2 tsp French's yellow mustard
- 1 C. brown sugar, packed
- 2 tbsp apple cider vinegar
- 1 1/2 tsp chili powder
- 1 tsp celery seed
- 2 tsp salt
- 1/2 tsp black pepper

Directions

1. Heat a large skillet and cook the beef till browned lightly.
2. Drain the excess grease from the skillet.
3. In a large pan, mix together the remaining ingredients on medium-low heat and cook for about 10-15 minutes.
4. Stir in the beef and onions and simmer for about 15 minutes.

CANADIAN
Blueberry Pie

🥣 Prep Time: 15 mins
⏲ Total Time: 50 mins

Servings per Recipe: 8
Calories   485.2
Fat   19.0
Cholesterol   30.8m
Sodium   320.1mg
Carbohydrates   75.0
Protein   5.7g

Ingredients

5 C. fresh blueberries
1 tbsp lemon juice
1 (15 oz.) packages refrigerated pie crusts
1 C. sugar
1/2 C. all-purpose flour
1/8 tsp salt
1/2 tsp ground cinnamon
2 tbsp butter
1 large egg, lightly beaten
1 tsp sugar

Directions

1. Set your oven to 400 degrees F before doing anything else.
2. In a bowl, add the berries and drizzle with the lemon juice and keep aside.
3. In a 9-inch pie plate, place half of the pastry according to package's directions.
4. In a bowl, mix together 1 C. of the sugar, flour, salt and cinnamon.
5. Add the flour mixture into the bowl with the berries and stir to combine.
6. Place the berry mixture into pastry shell and top with the butter in the shape of dots.
7. Unfold the remaining pastry onto a lightly floured surface and with the rolling pin, roll gently to remove creases.
8. Evenly.
9. Seal and crimp the edges.
10. Cut the slits in top of crust to let the steam to escape.
11. Brush the top of the pastry with beaten egg and sprinkle with 1 tsp of the sugar.
12. Cook in the oven for about 35 minutes.
13. Cover the edges with a piece of the foil to prevent over browning, if necessary.
14. Serve with a topping of the vanilla ice cream.

Southern American Pie

Prep Time: 20 mins
Total Time: 1 hr 20 mins

Servings per Recipe: 8
Calories   395.8
Fat   19.0
Cholesterol   101.4m
Sodium   269.8mg
Carbohydrates   52.2
Protein   5.0g

Ingredients

- 1/2 C. butter, melted
- 1 1/2 C. sugar
- 3 tbsp flour
- 3 eggs, beaten
- 1 pinch salt
- 1 tsp vanilla
- 1 C. buttermilk
- 1 deep dish pie shell (either your own recipe or store-bought)

Directions

1. Set your oven to 400 degrees F before doing anything else.
2. In a large bowl, add the butter and sugar and beat till light.
3. Add the eggs and beat well.
4. Add the vanilla and beat to combine.
5. In a bowl, sift together the flour and salt.
6. Add the flour mixture into the butter mixture alternatively with the buttermilk and beat till smooth.
7. Place the mixture into a deep dish pie shell evenly.
8. Cook in the oven for about 10 minutes.
9. Now, set the oven to 350 F and cook in the oven for about 50-60 minutes or till a toothpick inserted in the center comes out clean.

OLD-FASHIONED
American Pecan Pie

Prep Time: 10 mins
Total Time: 55 mins

Servings per Recipe: 6
Calories 653.4
Fat 37.4
Cholesterol 120.0m
Sodium 282.6mg
Carbohydrates 78.3
Protein 6.9g

Ingredients

3 eggs
1 C. corn syrup
1 tsp vanilla extract
1 1/4 C. pecan halves

2/3 C. sugar
1/3 C. butter (melted)
1 pie crust

Directions

1. Set your oven to 350 degrees F before doing anything else.
2. In a bowl, add the eggs and beat lightly.
3. Add the corn syrup, sugar, butter and vanilla extract and stir to combine well.
4. Stir in the pecan halves and place the filling into crust.
5. Cover the edges with a piece of the foil and cook in the oven for about 25 minutes.
6. Remove the piece of foil and cook in the oven for about 20 minutes.

Apple Pie

🥣 Prep Time: 10 mins
🕐 Total Time: 1 hr

Servings per Recipe: 8
Calories   405.5
Fat   15.4
Cholesterol   20.3m
Sodium   189.5mg
Carbohydrates   65.8
Protein   3.2g

Ingredients

1 ready-made pie crust
5 1/2 C. peeled cored sliced cooking apples
1 tbsp lemon juice
1/2 C. granulated sugar
1/4 C. brown sugar, packed
3 tbsp flour
1/2 tsp ground cinnamon
1/4 tsp allspice

Topping
3/4 C. flour
1/4 C. granulated sugar
1/4 C. brown sugar, packed
1/3 C. butter, room temperature

Directions

1. Set your oven to 375 degrees F before doing anything else.
2. Arrange the pie crust into the pie plate.
3. In a large bowl, mix together the sliced apples, lemon juice, both sugars, flour, cinnamon and allspice.
4. Place the apple mixture into the crust.
5. For topping in a medium bowl, add the flour, both sugars and butter and with a fork, mix till a coarse crumb mixture forms.
6. Sprinkle the crumb mixture over the apples evenly.
7. Cook in the oven for about 50 minutes.

SOUTHERN Georgia Peach Pie

Prep Time: 15 mins
Total Time: 1 hr 15 mins

Servings per Recipe: 8
Calories 432.5
Fat 17.5g
Cholesterol 69.2mg
Sodium 233.7mg
Carbohydrates 65.4g
Protein 5.3g

Ingredients

3 C. fresh peeled and chopped peaches
1 unbaked 9-inch deep dish pie pastry
1 C. sugar
1/3 C. all-purpose flour
1/8 tsp salt
2 eggs, beaten
1/2 C. sour cream

1/2 C. sugar
1/2 C. all-purpose flour
1/4 C. butter
1 fresh peach, sliced for garnish if desired

Directions

1. Set your oven to 350 degrees F before doing anything else.
2. Arrange 3 C. of the fresh peaches into a pie pastry.
3. In a bowl, mix together 1 C. of the sugar, 1/3 C. of the flour and salt.
4. Add the eggs and sour cream and mix till well combined.
5. Place the flour mixture over the peaches evenly.
6. In another bowl, add 1/2 C. of the sugar, 1/2 C. of the flour and 1/4 C. of the butter and with 2 forks, mix till a coarse meal like mixture forms.
7. Sprinkle the meal mixture over the pie evenly.
8. Cook in the oven for about 60 minutes.
9. Serve with a garnishing of the fresh peach slices.

American Sweet Corn

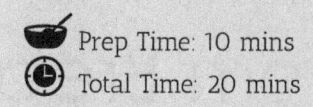

Prep Time: 10 mins
Total Time: 20 mins

Servings per Recipe: 8
Calories	253
Fat	16.5g
Cholesterol	54mg
Sodium	373mg
Carbohydrates	24.8g
Protein	5.1g

Ingredients

- 2 (10 oz.) packages frozen corn kernels, thawed
- 2 tbsp butter, softened
- 1 C. heavy cream
- 2 tbsp granulated sugar
- 1 tsp salt
- ¼ tsp freshly ground black pepper
- 2 tbsp all-purpose flour
- ¼ C. whole milk
- ¼ C. Parmesan cheese, grated freshly

Directions

1. In a large skillet, mix together corn, butter, cream, sugar, salt and black pepper on medium heat.
2. In a bowl, add flour and milk and beat till well combined.
3. Gradually, add flour mixture in skillet, beating continuously.
4. Cook, stirring continuously for about 3-5 minutes or till corns are cooked and sauce become thick.
5. Remove from heat and immediately add cheese and stir till melted completely.
6. Serve hot.

SOUTHERN
Corn Bread

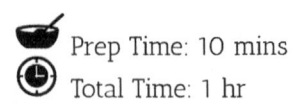

🍳 Prep Time: 10 mins
🕐 Total Time: 1 hr

Servings per Recipe: 6
Calories	587
Fat	36g
Cholesterol	138mg
Sodium	1317mg
Carbohydrates	54.6g
Protein	14.5g

Ingredients

1 (12 oz.) package corn bread mix
1 (8¾ oz.) can sweet corn, drained
1 (8 oz.) can cream-style corn
2 eggs, beaten
½ C. butter, melted

1 C. sour cream
1 C. Swiss cheese, shredded freshly

Directions

1. Set your oven to 350 degrees F. Grease an 8x8-inch baking pan.
2. In a large bowl, add all ingredients except cheese and mix till well combined.
3. Transfer the corn mixture into prepared baking pan.
4. Bake for about 35-40 minutes.
5. Remove the baking pan from oven. Top the bread with shredded cheese evenly.
6. Bake for 10 minutes more or till a toothpick inserted in the center comes out clean.
7. Serve warm.

Southern Corn Bread II

Prep Time: 15 mins
Total Time: 40 mins

Servings per Recipe: 9
Calories   241
Fat   11.6 g
Cholesterol   46 mg
Sodium   289 mg
Carbohydrates   29.9 g
Protein   4.4 g

Ingredients

1 C. cornmeal
1 C. all-purpose flour
½ tsp baking soda
½ tsp baking powder
½ tsp salt
¼ C. white sugar
1 egg, beaten lightly
1/3 C. milk
1 C. sour cream
¼ C. butter, melted

Directions

1. Set your oven to 400 degrees F. Lightly, grease an 8-inch square baking pan.
2. In a large bowl, mix together cornmeal, flour, baking soda, baking powder and salt.
3. In another bowl, add white sugar, egg, milk, cream and butter and beat till well combined.
4. Mix egg mixture into flour mixture completely.
5. Place the bread mixture in prepared baking pan evenly.
6. Bake for about 20-25 minutes or till a tooth pick inserted in the center of cake comes out clean.
7. Serve warm.

CAESAR
Parmesan Pasta Salad

 Prep Time: 15 mins
 Total Time: 30 mins

Servings per Recipe: 12
Calories	291 kcal
Carbohydrates	32.6 g
Cholesterol	6 mg
Fat	14.6 g
Protein	8.5 g
Sodium	728 mg

Ingredients

- 1 (16 ounce) package rotini pasta
- 1 cup Italian-style salad dressing
- 1 cup creamy Caesar salad dressing
- 1 cup grated Parmesan cheese
- 1 red bell pepper, diced
- 1 green bell pepper, chopped
- 1 red onion, diced

Directions

1. Cook pasta in salty boiling water for about 10 minutes until tender before draining it.
2. Mix pasta, red bell pepper, Italian salad dressing, Caesar dressing, Parmesan cheese, green bell pepper and red onion very thoroughly before refrigerating for a few hours.
3. Serve.

Garden Party Pasta Salad

Prep Time: 15 mins
Total Time: 30 mins

Servings per Recipe: 12
Calories	289 kcal
Carbohydrates	34.6 g
Cholesterol	8 mg
Fat	13.9 g
Protein	10 g
Sodium	764 mg

Ingredients

1 (16 ounce) package uncooked rotini pasta
1 (16 ounce) bottle Italian salad dressing
2 cucumbers, chopped
6 tomatoes, chopped
1 bunch green onions, chopped
4 ounces grated Parmesan cheese
1 tbsp Italian seasoning

Directions

1. Cook pasta in salty boiling water for about 10 minutes until tender before draining it.
2. Coat a mixture of pasta, green onions, cucumbers and tomatoes with a mixture of parmesan cheese and Italian seasoning very thoroughly before refrigerating it covered for a few hours.
3. Serve.

FUSILLI
and Mushrooms

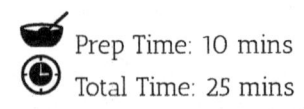

🥣 Prep Time: 10 mins
🕐 Total Time: 25 mins

Servings per Recipe: 8
Calories			181 kcal
Carbohydrates		38.1 g
Cholesterol		0 mg
Fat			0.7 g
Protein			5.4 g
Sodium			238 mg

Ingredients

10 ounces fusilli pasta
1 onion, chopped
1 green bell pepper, chopped
2 tomatoes, chopped

1 cup chopped mushrooms
3/4 cup fat free Italian-style dressing

Directions

1. Cook pasta in salty boiling water for about 10 minutes until tender before draining it.
2. Mix pasta, mushrooms, onions, tomatoes and bell pepper very thoroughly before refrigerating for at least one hour.
3. Serve.

Grilled Pasta Salad

Prep Time: 15 mins
Total Time: 45 mins

Servings per Recipe: 4
Calories   504 kcal
Carbohydrates   48 g
Cholesterol   103 mg
Fat   13.2 g
Protein   46.5 g
Sodium   650 mg

Ingredients

4 skinless, boneless chicken breast halves
steak seasoning to taste
8 ounces rotini pasta
8 ounces mozzarella cheese, cubed
1 red onion, chopped
1 head romaine lettuce, chopped
6 cherry tomatoes, chopped

Directions

1. At first you need to set grill at medium heat and put some oil before starting anything else.
2. Coat chicken breast with steak seasoning before cooking it on the preheated grill for 8 minutes each side.
3. Cook pasta in salty boiling water for about 10 minutes until tender before draining it.
4. Add mixture of tomatoes, cheese, onion and lettuce into the bowl containing pasta and chicken.
5. Mix it thoroughly before serving.